# Myths & Legends of the

# Indians

## of the

# Southwest

By Bertha Dutton & Caroline Olin

Book II

# Hopi, Acoma, Tewa, Zuni

(Book I, Myths & Legends of the Navajo, Pima, Apache, is also available.)

Mask of Hehea.

After Stevenson.

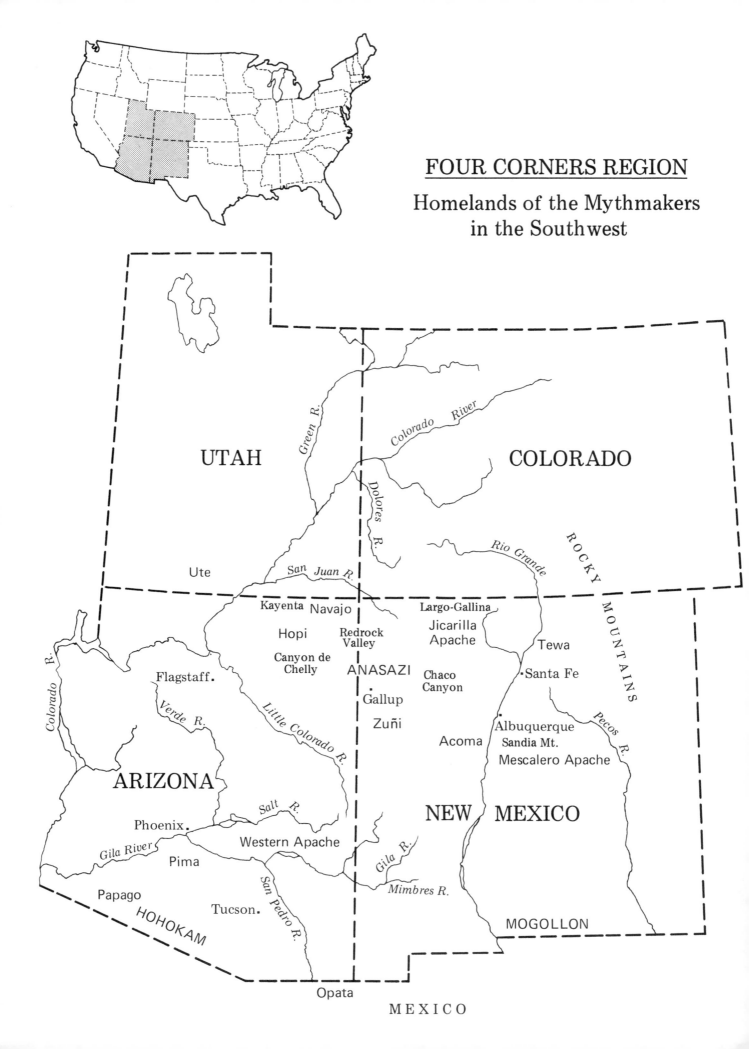

# FOUR CORNERS REGION

Homelands of the Mythmakers
in the Southwest

UTAH

COLORADO

*Green R.*

*Colorado River*

*Dolores R.*

*Rio Grande*

ROCKY MOUNTAINS

Ute

*San Juan R.*

Kayenta  Navajo

Largo-Gallina

Hopi

Redrock
Valley

Jicarilla
Apache

Tewa

Canyon de
Chelly

ANASAZI

Chaco
Canyon

Santa Fe

Flagstaff.

*Colorado R.*

*Verde R.*

*Little Colorado R.*

Gallup

Zuñi

Albuquerque
Sandia Mt.
Mescalero Apache

*Pecos R.*

Acoma

ARIZONA

*Salt R.*

NEW MEXICO

Phoenix.

Western Apache

*Gila River*

Pima

*Gila R.*

*San Pedro R.*

*Mimbres R.*

Papago

HOHOKAM

Tucson.

MOGOLLON

Opata

MEXICO

# THE PUEBLO INDIANS

Because of their outstanding architectural remains and rich accumulations of artifacts, the ruins of the Four Corners Region have been known for many years. Spanish explorers who came into the Southwest in 1540 and thereafter, called the house-dwelling natives "Pueblo Indians," and their settlements *pueblos*, for they were similar to the homes and villages they had left in Spain.

The Spaniards learned that the Pueblo Indians had two types of organization. Ceremonial duties were controlled by a "priest-chief," the Sun-watcher—whom they called *cacique*. The head of a civil, or secular, body—who served as an intermediary between the cacique and the public—was called "governor."

Archaeologists studying the ancient ruins found many connections between the peoples who had inhabited them and the modern Pueblo Indians—who are known today as 19 distinct Pueblo groups. (Each one is an entity independent of the others. Eighteen of them are in New Mexico, mostly in the Rio Grande drainage. One group, the Hopi, dwells in northeastern Arizona. *See* Map). Archaeologists adopted the term "Anasazi" for referring to "those who had gone before"—the Ancient Pueblos.

Knowledge gained from excavations of the ruins and from comparisons with living Indian cultures has revealed that many traits and practices entered the Southwest from countries to the south—from Mesoamerica. Certain architectural ideas and ceremonial items indicate that the Hohokam, Mogollon, and Pueblo societies were strongly affected by southern Indians.

Aboriginal Southwestern peoples commonly believed that humans, animals, birds, trees, objects, fire, water—everything—possessed magical powers. They lived and they could talk. As the cultures developed and were modified by incoming influences, cults, priesthoods, and secret societies were organized and strictly controlled. All dealt with things of most concern to the Indians: rain making, fertility, healing, warfare, and child training. Particularly among the western pueblos, including Zuñi, the Hopi villages, Acoma, and Laguna—wherein all were farmers concerned with weather control—rain making and well-being were all-important. One of the prominent societies was related to "the spirit rain makers," who appear in the guise of kátsinas.

Mythical fish

From a Mimbres bowl in the Museum of New Mexico, Santa Fe

This water color painting was made many years ago by a young school boy of his home pueblo, Zuñi. It is his portrayal of the original War God of the Zuñi, with whom the Twin War Gods were closely associated. The central figure, called the Knife Wing God, is shown in human form with wings and tail of a great bird. His terraced altar headdress represents his dwelling place among the clouds. His ornaments and attire are those of the Kóko. Weapons of this culture hero are a great stone knife of war, the rainbow, and arrows of lightning. Clouds and celestial symbols adorn the wall of the chamber in which the painting is shown, presumably the Priesthood of the Bow.

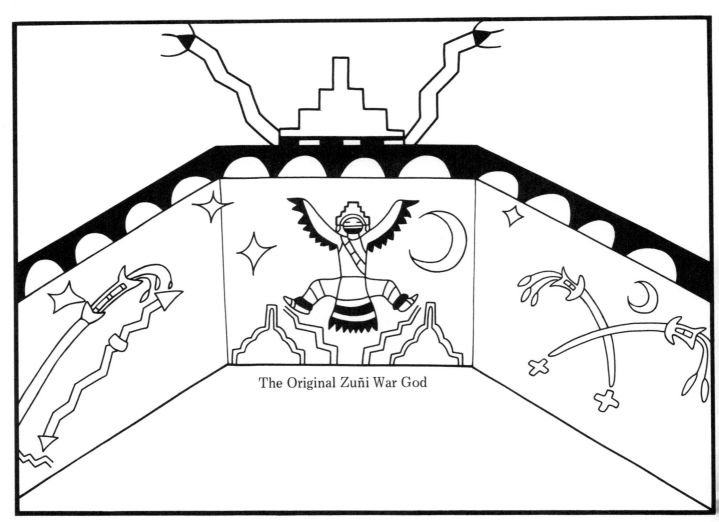

The Original Zuñi War God

From a painting by a Zuñi school boy

Mask of *Nátashku*
After M. Stevenson, 1904, Pl. LXXI

# THE INDIANS OF ZUÑI
## The Kóko—Spirit People

The Indians of Zuñi, who live in a pueblo south of Gallup, New Mexico, have been able to continue many of the ancient ways right up to the present. Every aspect of Zuñi life is integrated: individual and community affairs, daily work, ceremonialism, arts and crafts. The Zuñi believe that all things in nature have a soul, and that mankind must live in harmony with nature.

A colorful body of spirit people comprise a mythic drama-dance organization known as *kóko*. The kóko correspond to the commonly called kátsinas of the Rio Grande and Hopi pueblos. Kóko personages are impersonated by humans who perform many duties, such as training the children in the Zuñi way of life, and rain making.

Beautiful kóko groups take part in ceremonial rites and elaborate dances. Accompanying them may be members of priest-clown societies, whose members are curious beings, neither male nor female, but "formed as the potter forms clay." The Mud Heads are members of one such society.

Twelve in number, they were born of hideous parents. Even though silly, they were as wise as the deities and high priests—for simpletons often utter wise words and prophecy. Sometimes they are thought to be married to the kóko, the Old Ones.

*Kóloowisi*, Zuñi plumed serpent effigy
After M. Stevenson, 1904, Pl. XIII

# The Beginning of the World

According to Zuñi tradition, Earth-mother and Sky-father were changeable, even as smoke in the wind. They could manifest themselves in any form at will, as dancers may by wearing masks.

They changed themselves into a man and a woman. "Behold!" said the Earth-mother as a great terraced bowl filled with water appeared. "This shall be like the homes of my tiny children. On the rim of each world-country in which they wander, terraced mountains shall stand, separating country from country.

Zuñi Eagle Dancer

From an Indian painting in the Museum of New Mexico, Santa Fe

"Behold again!" she said as she spat on the water, smiting and stirring it with her fingers. Foam gathered about the terraced rim, mounting higher. "Yea," she said, "and from my bosom they shall draw liquid nourishment." Then with her warm breath she blew across the terraces. White flecks of the foam broke away, and, floating above the water, were shattered by the cold breath of the Sky-father. Fine mist and spray shed abundantly down.

"Even so," she said, "shall white clouds float up from the great waters at the borders of the world, and clustering about the mountain terraces be borne aloft by the breaths of soul-beings, and of our children. Clouds shall be hardened and broken by Sky-father's cold, shedding downward in rain spray, the water of life, into the hollow places of my lap. For therein shall nestle our children, mankind and creature kind, for warmth from thy coldness.

"Lo," said Earth-mother, "even the trees on high mountains near clouds and Sky-father crouch low toward Earth-mother for warmth and protection! Warm is Earth-mother, cold is Sky-father, even as woman is the warm, and man the cold being!"

Then Sky-father spoke. "Not alone," he said, "shalt thou be helpful unto our children, for behold." And he spread his hand abroad with the palm downward. Into all the wrinkles and crevices thereof he set what-seemed-to-be yellow corn grains. In the dark of the early world-dawn they gleamed like sparks of fire, moving as his hand was moved over the bowl, shining up from the depths of the water. "See," he said, pointing to the seven grains clasped by his thumb and four fingers, "by these seven seed stars shall our children be guided.

"When the Sun-father is not here," he continued, "and thy terraces are dark, then shall our children be guided by lights—in and around the midmost place, where our children shall abide. Yea, and even as these grains gleam up from the water, so shall numberless seed-grains spring up from thy bosom when touched by my waters, to nourish our children."

Thus and in other ways they took care of their offspring.

Zuñi ceremonial fixtures (sides) and fetish of *Shíwanni* (Rain Priest) of Black Corn Clan (bottom)

After M. Stevenson, 1904, Pl. XXXVI

## People and Other Creatures Formed

In the deepest of the four cave-wombs of the world, the seed of men and other creatures took form and increased—just as worms which appear within eggs soon burst their shells and become birds, tadpoles or serpents—even mankind.

Thus the lowermost cave-womb, black as a chimney at night and foul, too, overfilled with being. Everywhere unfinished creatures crawled like reptiles over one another in filth and black darkness, crowding together and stepping on each other, spitting and doing other indecencies. Their murmurings and wailings grew so loud that many sought to escape, growing wiser and more manlike.

Then Póshaiyangkya, the wisest of wise men and all-sacred master, rose from the lowermost sea. Pitying men, he tried to lead them up from that first cave-womb. But the ways were so dark and narrow that those who crowded after could not follow. Alone, then, he climbed up from one cave to another, out into the breadth of daylight. There the earth lay like an island in the midst of the waters, wet and unstable. Alone he sought the Sun-father, and asked him to deliver mankind and the creatures below.

"Then did the Sun-father take counsel with himself, and casting his glance downward discovered, on the great waters, a foam-cap near the Earth-mother. With his beam he impregnated and with his heat warmed the foam-cap, whereupon Earth-mother gave birth to the Beloved Two, Twin Brothers of Light, yet one elder and one younger, as close as question and answer in deciding and doing."

With them the Sun-father shared thought control and his own knowledge-wisdom. He gave them the great cloud-bow, and for arrows the thunderbolts of the four quarters, two to either. He gave them the fog-making shield, spun of spray and the floating clouds, supported on the wind, yet hiding its bearer. And he gave them the management of men and all creatures.

Well instructed by the Sun-father, the Beloved Two lifted him with their great cloud-bow into the vault of the sky, that the earth might become warm and more fit for men and the creatures. Then along the trail of the sun-seeking Póshaiyangkya, they sped backward on their floating fog-shield to the Mountain of Generation. With magic knives they spread open the depths of the mountain. Still on their cloud-shield they descended into the dark of the under-world, even as a spider crawls down the funnel of her web.

There they lived with men and the creatures, seeking ways to lead them forth.

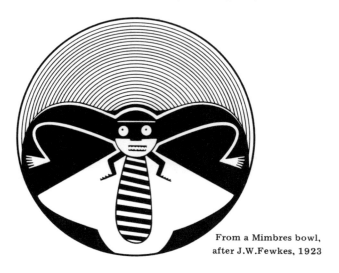

From a Mimbres bowl,
after J.W.Fewkes, 1923

## Ladder of Grass

Now in the depths of the cave-womb grasses were growing, and crawling vines. So the Beloved Two breathed on the stems of these grasses, causing them to grow by walking round them and twisting them upward until lo! they reached up into the light. And from where they grasped the stems, branching leaves sprang forth. With these the Beloved Two formed a ladder, up which men and the creatures might climb to the second cave-floor.

Up this ladder crowded men and the creatures, following the Beloved Two. "Yet many fell back and, lost in the darkness, peopled the under-world, becoming the monsters and deformed beings of olden time." In the second cave-womb it was dark as a night in a storm, but larger and higher than the first because it was nearer the navel of the Earth-mother. Thus it was called the Place of Gestation.

Here again men and the creatures increased, and their complainings grew loud and beseeching. Again the Two, helping the great ladder to grow, guided them upward, this time not all at once, "but in successive bands to become the six kinds of men," (the yellow, the tawny gray, the red, the white, the mingled, and the black races.) Multitudes were lost or left behind.

A Great Horned-toad Medicine Band at Zuñi

after F.H. Cushing, 1974, Pl.XXIV

The third great cave-womb, where men and the creatures had now come, was larger and higher than the second, and much lighter, like a valley in starlight. It was "named the Place of Sex-generation. For here the various peoples and beings began to multiply apart from one another. As the nations and tribes of men and the creatures waxed numerous, the third cave-womb became overfilled. As before, generations of nations were led out successively, with many lost or left behind, into the next and last cave-womb, the Place of Parturition, from which birth occurs."

Here it was light like the dawning. Men began to learn variously according to their natures. The Beloved Two taught them to seek first of all the Sun-father. He would, they said, reveal to them knowledge of the ways of life.

Yet as in the other cave-wombs, this, too, became crowded with beings. At successive periods, the Two finally led the nations of men and the creatures into the great upper world, which is called the World of Knowledge and Seeing.

A shelter in a Corn Field, high *mesas* in the background

After F.H. Cushing, 1974, Pl.V

A Zuñi Altar of the Great Fire Fraternity

After M. Stevenson, 1904, Pl. CXVI

## Men in the World of Light

Eight years made the span of four days and four nights when the world was new. Men and the creatures were nearer alike then than now. Men were black, like the caves they came out of. Their skins were cold and scaly like those of mud-creatures, their eyes were goggled like those of an owl, their ears were membranous like those of cave-bats, their feet were webbed like those of alligators, and they had tails. Often they crawled along like toads, lizards, and newts.

Like infants who fear to walk straight, they crouched as they had in their cave-worlds, that they might not stumble and fall in the uncertain light. And when the morning star rose they blinked excessively as they beheld its brightness, crying out that surely the Sun-father was coming. But it was only the elder of the Beloved Two, heralding with his shield of flame the approach of Sun-father.

When in the east the Sun-father himself appeared, though shrouded in the midst of the great world waters, they were so blinded and heated by his glory that they cried out to one another and fell down wallowing, covering their eyes with their bare hands and arms. Yet ever anew they looked afresh at the sun and struggled towards it, as moths and other night creatures seek the light of a camp fire, even though they may burn.

At last they became used to the light, and to the high world they had entered, and no longer walked bended. It was then that they girded themselves with bark and rushes. By thus walking only on their hind feet, the same became bruised and sore. They sought to protect them with sandals of yucca fiber.

It was thus, by much invention, that men began to know things, and were instructed by what they saw, and so became wiser and better able to receive the words and gifts of their fathers and elder brothers, the gods, the Beloved Two, and priests. In the light of the Sun-father, persons became known from persons, and things from other things.

(Note: the preceding stories adapted from Cushing, F.H., "Outlines of Zuñi Creation," 13th Annual Report, Bureau of Ethnology, 1891-1892)

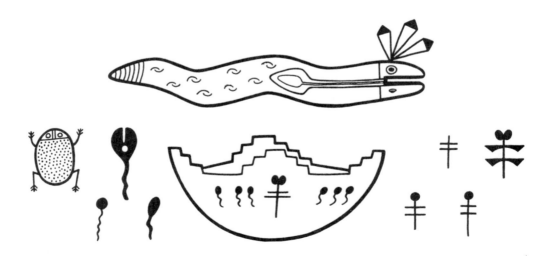

A water serpent, a terraced bowl representing Mother Earth,
and pond creatures: frog, tadpoles, dragonflies

Zuñi Mask of *Hémishiikwe*, tablet headdress on which Sun is represented

After M. Stevenson
1904, Pl. LXXIV

*Shúlawitsi,* Zuñi young Fire god

After M. Stevenson, 1904, Pl. LXII

Mask of *Múluktakia,* one of the most attractive *kóko* of the Zuñi

After M. Stevenson, 1904, Pl. LXXIII

*Zuñi Sáyatashe*, or Longhorn,
Rain priest of the North kiva

After M. Stevenson, 1904, Pl. LXIII

A Zuñi *Yámuhakto:* two of these,
representing the east and west, are
assistants of the gods
After M. Stevenson, 1904, Pl. LV

*Shálako,* A giant-sized messenger of the Zuñi rain gods

## The Story of the Salt Mother

A man called Turquois came to Zuñi from the Rio Grande pueblo of Santo Domingo. He was unhappy with the treatment given him in his home pueblo, and told Máwe, the Zuñi Salt Mother, of his troubles and his desire to go far away.

The war gods, the Beloved Two, overheard the conversation and said, "Mother, if you go far away you will be of much greater value, and we will go with you."

Leaving her home in the rocks in charge of the Frog clan, Máwe, Turquois Man, and the Beloved Two moved onward. Máwe and Turquois Man assumed the form of birds and flew to a beautiful lake. There the war gods decided they had gone far enough. Máwe agreed to stop, but Turquois Man journeyed southwest to make his home on a high mountain protected by angry white and black bears.

Some Indians believe that Máwe became the salt lake south of Zuñi, which belonged to the Parrot clan.

Salt is much desired by the Indians. Since Máwe's transformation, the Parrot clan at the pueblo of Laguna has had sole charge of the pilgrimages made to the lake. Laguna people say that the Zuñi, as well as the Hopi, did not know how to get the salt before the Laguna showed them the proper observances.

The pilgrimages are carried on ritually. No filth of any kind is permitted in the region. Prayer sticks are prepared as an offering to the Salt Mother, and participants in the ceremony cleanse their bodies before they go into the lake to get salt. This is a solemn occasion. It is only with many prayers that Salt Mother gives up her salt. When any lack of proper observances occurs, the salt remains in solution so that it cannot be secured. But when Salt Mother is in a good mood, the salt is hardened and may be gathered in large sheets.

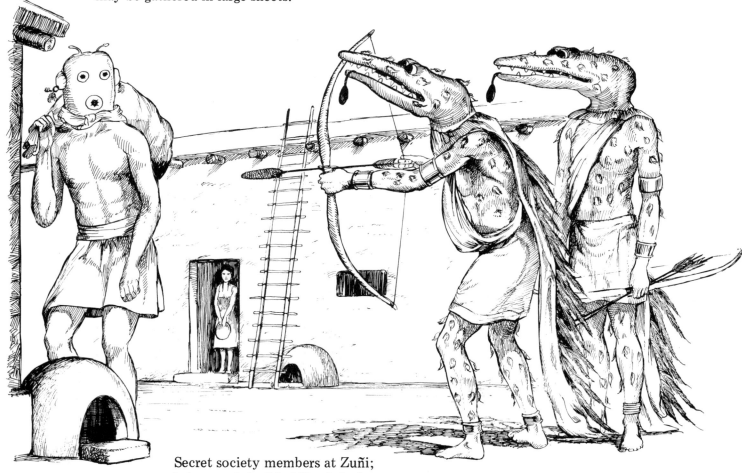

Secret society members at Zuñi;
at left one of the Mud Heads is shown
After F.H. Cushing, 1974:625

When the salt is brought back, it must be blessed before it can be used. The pilgrims gather at one home for each clan. Relatives perform purification rites over the pilgrims and wash their hair in yucca suds. Women members of each clan do the washing, each woman giving each man's head a few rubs. Then they bless them with corn, asking for long life.

A Zuñi Little Dancer: Double Face.

After R. Bunzel, 1932

Zuñi Corn Maidens dancing.

After M. Stevenson, 1904, Pl. XXXIX

A Zuñi Little Dancer: *Náhalico*, Crazy Grandchild

After R. Bunzel, 1932

# THE INDIANS OF HOPILAND

The Hopi (HO-pee) are a composite of Indian peoples who moved into northeastern Arizona centuries ago. Originally clans were significant among them. A certain clan in its travels found a dead bear upon which the members gazed, "and from that they were called forever afterwards the Bear clan." That clan came to Hopiland at an early date from the Rio Grande valley in New Mexico, bringing the Tewa language and many customs with them. Peoples who came from the north and south spoke another tongue. Hopi pueblos were built on three high *mesas*, or plateaus: First Mesa in the east, Second Mesa in the middle, and Third Mesa in the west.

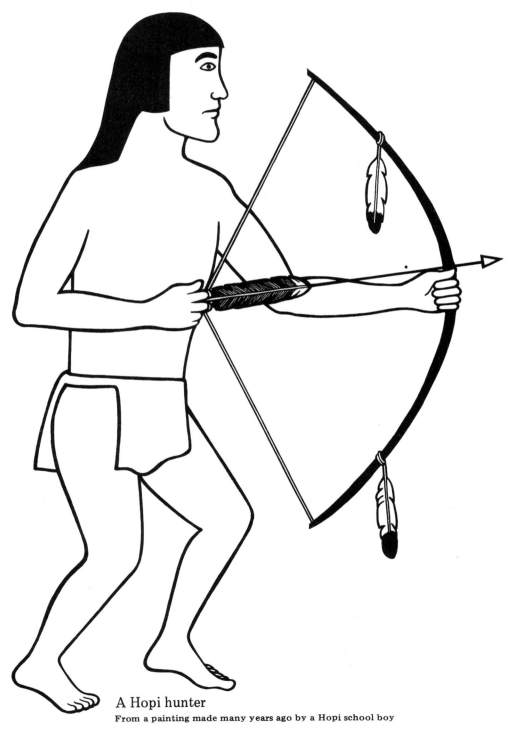

A Hopi hunter

From a painting made many years ago by a Hopi school boy

According to Hopi beliefs, the game animals are considered as people. Their mother was a female deity, *Tíkuoi Wuuti*, or the Outcast Woman, turned away by the Hopi during their legendary migrations. The father was the earth deity, *Masao*, dweller on the earth surface and underground. As ruler of the underworld he is the deity of death.

A Hopi story teller has said that his people believe animals have homes "like kivas" the world over, and when they need rest they convert themselves into human beings and live in these places. To gain their confidence, at dawn a Hopi goes to the game animals, asking for their mercy. He says that he wishes to eat them for food and would like to be chosen as their god-father and allowed to catch them at the time of the hunt.

The deer, antelope, and mountain sheep are easily convinced that this should be, but the cottontails and jackrabbits are not readily pursuaded. These are among many animals impersonated in the kátsina ceremonies.

### The Magic of the Kátsinas

The Hopi believe that souls of good people turn into kátsinas and become associated with clouds. In this guise they can bring rain, the greatest of all material benefits to the Hopi. The kátsina cult is closely linked to the cult of the dead, which serves to explain why their ceremonies are limited to one-half of the calendar year, for they are supposed to spend the other half in the spirit world. Only Masao, the kátsina related to the god of death, may appear during the closed season.

When a human invests himself with the paraphernalia of a kátsina, he *becomes* the supernatural one. He relives the folk history and mythology of the culture hero represented. No longer does he speak with mankind.

A several-day-and-night ceremonial called Pówamu is the major event of the Hopi kátsina cult. Its purpose is to promote germination and fertility. An impressive ritual is the planting of beans in the kivas. The Pówamu chief brings prayer sticks to the kiva chiefs. Each of them selects a member who is given a prayer feather and instructed to gather soil in which the beans are to be planted. The Sand clan is keeper of the soil. After permission is secured, the men go to a specified spot for the sanctified earth. There they plant prayer sticks and pray for the beans' rapid growth. The soil is taken then to their kivas, placed in earthen vessels, and the beans are planted.

*Wénima*, land of the dead, carvings (petroglyphs) on a rock cliff in Hopiland

An unmasked Bean dancer of the Hopi

From an Indian painting in the Museum of New Mexico

Intense heat in the kivas, careful watering, and rituals solemnly enacted, force growth. About the eighth day, young plants begin to appear. This in the cold of winter, usually in February, seems a miracle indeed. When hundreds of bean plants, and a few blades of corn planted by Eótoto, Father of the Kátsinas, have sprouted, unmasked kátsina dancers in magnificent attire visit the kivas. They participate in purification rites to help the plants grow.

After the bean dance, the kátsinas return to their spirit world atop the San Francisco Peaks north of Flagstaff. The season is closed.

**Sun and Spider Woman, grandmother of the Twin War Gods**
After J.W. Fewkes, 1919, Pl.87

## Pookong Kills a Bear

One of the Hopi stories tells that in a middle mesa village there lived a boy called *Pookong* with his grandmother in one of the kátsina houses. A bear was killing the village people. The unhappy chief wondered what to do. Finally he decided to send Pookong after the bear. He made Pookong a bow of hard wood and arrows adorned with parrot feathers. On one of the arrows he added bluebird feathers. He made a ball cut from buckskin, sewed together and stuffed with cotton. He rubbed red ochre on the ball. For the grandmother he made a prayerstick.

When the ball and prayer stick were finished, the chief took them to the house of Pookong. This made the grandmother happy. The chief handed the ball, bow and arrows to Pookong, saying, "With these you kill the bear, because I have made them for you."

Pookong was happy. He went to hunt the bear just as the bear was walking around hunting for someone else. The two met. The bear stood, holding up his great paws. Pookong knelt and aimed. He shot and hit it in the throat. When the bear fell, he hit it with the ball and the bear died.

Pookong skinned the bear, legs first, but did not cut the abdomen. He left the skin in the form of a bag, pulling it over his head like a shirt. From the feet he cut off the claws. He filled the skin with dry grass. Oh! it looked like an ugly bear. He tied a woolen rope around its neck, then around himself. Dragging it behind him, he ran very fast, screaming, "Uhu, a bear is following me!"

Pueblo of Walpi on First Mesa, Hopiland
After V. Mindeleff, 1891: Pl. XXIII

"Why, he's right," the people cried, and they ran, too. They told the grandmother, "A bear is after your grandchild." The grandmother ran crying into her kiva.

Then Pookong came to the house and threw the stuffed bear skin at the grandmother. Because she was so scared, she died at once. Pookong laughed at the grandmother and kicked her. "Get up," he commanded, and the grandmother woke. When she sat up she caught and whipped Pookong. "You are naughty, you have scared me," she cried. But the chief was very happy and forever after the village lived in peace.

A Tewa Bear dancer
(a man wearing a bear skin to represent that animal in a dance)
From an Indian painting in the Museum of New Mexico

Little War God, the elder of the twins common to the Pueblo peoples    After J. W. Fewkes, 1903

Little War God, the younger of the twins common to the Pueblo peoples

After J. W. Fewkes, 1903

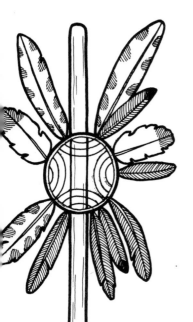

Ceremonial fixture
for the altar of the
Twin War Gods
After M. Stevenson, 1904

## THE ACOMA INDIANS
### Meeting the Spirit Rainmakers

Among the Pueblo Indians who say they originated in the north are the Keres of Acoma *(AH-co-mah)*. They now live some fifty miles west of Albuquerque. They say that they came with their mother *Iatiku*, through a hole in the north called *Shípap*.

There was a lake, with an island in the middle and a large sanctuary on it. Their mother Iatiku taught them everything. Then, when they were able to care for themselves, she went to live in that building. She promised that she would always be near by to help them and to take care of them.

Iatiku told the people about the kátsina, who lived out west at *Wénimatsi*. She told them that they must respect these spirit people—spirit rain makers—for they were very powerful. She said they would come and dance for the people. Two brothers, very powerful and very wise, became the leaders of the people. These were Masewi and Oyoyewi, the twin war gods.

According to the Acoma, two scouts came one day and announced that the kátsina were coming in four days. Everyone busied themselves. The women ground corn and made bread; the men hunted rabbits and deer. Masewi and Oyoyewi showed the people how to make prayer sticks and how to revere the kátsina. On the evening of the third day, the people prayed to the kátsina with their prayer sticks and corn meal and made offerings of bread and game. The next morning, preceded by two scouts, the kátsina arrived. They were attired like masked dancers are today, but they wore no masks;"their faces looked the way the masks do today."

They came into the pueblo plaza."Masewi and his brother went forward to meet them, handing them bunches of prayer sticks. The other people were close behind and they, too, met the kátsina. Then the kátsina distributed presents. They carried small buckskin bags with them. When they were opened and their contents discharged they became magnified and multiplied manifold. They had bows and arrows, clothing (for the people were still naked), pottery, flints, buckskins, and tools, which they distributed to the people. The kátsina instructed the people in the uses of all the gifts, and they made inquiries regarding the clans."

"Then Masewi and Oyoyewi told the people that they must 'believe in the kátsina,' that they were powerful, that they were rain-makers. Then the kátsina began to dance in the plaza. They danced all day. In the evening they left, returning to Wénimatsi, their home in the west. The scouts told the people, before leaving, that if they wanted the kátsina to return they should make prayer sticks and to worship them.

After an original painting of a running deer by a Keres Indian artist

In each case the scouts would come to announce the kátsina four days before their arrival.

"Then the Acoma people were happy. They had food, tools, clothing, and weapons. When they became bored or lonesome they had the kátsina come to dance for them. They had learned many things, hunting, a few games, etc. They made herb-brew which they used as an emetic..."

Pueblo Prayer Stick
After M. Stevenson, 1904

## The Battle with the Kátsina

After a time, the Acoma decided to move from Shípap, for it was a very sacred place and they feared they might spoil it. So Masewi decided to move them to White House which lay to the south.

"When they had become established in their new home they decided to try to call the kátsina, for they were not sure that they would come to their new home. So they made prayer sticks and worshipped as they had been taught. The scouts came, followed after four days by the kátsina."

In the evening, after one of their dances, the people were gathered in a large room to play hidden ball. Everyone was happy. One warrior mimicked the peculiarities of the kátsina. Everyone laughed. Then others gave comic imitations, which caused great merriment.

Suddenly someone left the room. It was a kátsina who had been sitting there all the time. The people tried to catch him, but he had disappeared when they reached the door. He returned to Wénimatsi to tell his fellows.

The kátsina were very angry. They decided to return to White House and destroy the village. That night the war cry "Ah-a-a-a-a-a Ai!" alarmed all the Acoma. Masewi and his brother went out. They met four scouts from Wénimatsi who told the brothers that the kátsina were going to come and kill everyone. Masewi and Oyoyewi began preparing for defense. They got poles and skins and made a barricade.

"The following morning thousands of kátsina were seen running toward White House from the west, raising a big cloud of dust. They were met by the people of the village, the women behind, the men in front. Many people were killed, but if a kátsina was killed he immediately came to life again and resumed fighting. At nightfall the fighting ceased and the kátsina returned to Wénimatsi. The remaining people not dead were very sad. They quarreled among themselves, blaming each other for their misfortune."

"The next day the scouts returned from Wénimatsi. They told the people that they could never see the kátsina again. If, however, they wished them to come in spirit they should dress just like the kátsina, pray in the usual way, and then impersonate the kátsina in their dances."

(Note: these stories are adapted from White, L.A., 47th Annual Report, Bureau of American Ethnology, 1932).

## Impersonating the Kátsina

A month or two passed, when Masewi summoned the Acoma together to talk again about the kátsina. They decided to impersonate the kátsina as they had been directed by the scouts. So Masewi and his brother began to make masks. But many people were skeptical; they did not think that impersonation would be effective.

With six or eight men the two brothers prepared six to eight masks to represent kátsina. Then they built a house in which to practice songs and dances.

"Early one morning two men, dressed as scouts, left the village and went out west. At daybreak they returned to the village. The people who were ignorant of the scheme were very frightened; they feared another attack. Masewi and his brother met the scouts in the plaza. The scouts said that the kátsina would come to visit them in four days. Everyone was glad and set about making preparations for their reception. Peace was to be made. On the third day Masewi appointed three war chiefs—a head chief and two lieutenants—and told them how to receive the kátsina.

On the morning of the fourth day two scouts again arrived in the village,

Corn grinding for the
winter and summer
Masked dances
After R. Bunzel, 1932

Zuñi Prayer Stick
After M. Stevenson, 1904

followed by six or eight Indians dressed as kátsina. The war chiefs met them and made them welcome. They told the people about the wrong done the kátsina, and how they must be respected now. The masked Indians danced all day and at sunset walked back in the direction of Wénimatsi.

But the people could not agree among themselves; some thought it unwise to impersonate these spirit beings. Dissension spread in the village. Little bands detached themselves from the main body and migrated in various directions. Many, however, stayed behind, following the advice of Masewi. It was during these days of discord, too, that Mother Iatiku caused the people to speak different languages so that they could not quarrel with each other."

## The Crow and Parrot Eggs

Now Masewi, the leader of the Acoma who stayed behind, had two eggs, a parrot egg and a crow egg. One was blue and the other was white, but no one knew which was the parrot's egg. Masewi decided to lead his people to the south, where lay a place called *Áko* (the pueblo Acoma). He wished to go there and raise parrots. So they set out. In their wanderings they paused at various mesas, thinking perhaps that they had found Áko. Masewi's plan was to call out in a loud voice, "Aaaakoooo-o-o". If the echo sounded favorable they would settle there. But if the echo was not good they would pass on.

As they wandered, they stopped at several places now occupied by pueblos or ruin sites. One was too small a place to raise parrots. Always they traveled south. At a high butte, now called Enchanted Mesa, some stopped and made their home. Others followed Masewi southward.

"When they came to the east point of Acoma, Masewi called out, 'Aaaakoooo-o-o!' and received a perfect echo. 'This is Áko,' he announced. Then Masewi held up the two eggs, the blue and the white egg. The people divided themselves, some preferring the blue egg, others the white one, but both parties were of course trying to select the parrot egg.

"Most of the people chose the blue egg, so Masewi threw it against the cliff. Swarms of crows flew out. Those who had chosen this blue egg were sadly disappointed, but they had agreed to remain at Áko. Those who had chosen the white egg went on farther south, carrying the egg with them."

At their new homesite at Áko, the blue-egg people prepared to have the kátsina come, as they had done before. The scouts announced the arrival of the kátsina four days hence. They told the people to clean up the whole village, grind corn, bake bread and hunt game. They were to make a food sacrifice to the kátsina. The older people knew that the kátsina were merely impersonations, but the younger folks thought that the real kátsina were to come.

On the morning of the fourth day the Indians dressed like kátsina, preceded by the scouts, came. The war chief met them in the plaza. But they brought no presents, and never spoke, as they had done before the fatal battle. They danced in the plaza and prayed for rain. Rain came. Thus this ceremony became sacred and was repeated, and the masks were carefully preserved.

A group of Masked Dancers

From a painting by
a Zuñi school boy

# THE TEWA INDIANS

## The Tewa Emerge from Sand Lake

Three Indian groups living along the Rio Grande north of Santa Fe, New Mexico, speak the Tewa tongue. Tewa (TAY-wah) belongs to the Tanoan language family. These people, like the Keres-speaking Indians who dwell south of Santa Fe and westward to include Laguna and Acoma pueblos, believe they came into the Southwest from the north.

According to Tewa legends, a great many people were assembled under Sand Lake in an extensive dune area considered to be in southern Colorado. There they were seeking to find a place of emergence. There White Corn Mother, their summer mother was born. Four days later their Ice Mother, or winter mother, was born at the site of a little green grass. Then a man-woman (an all-including one) was brought into their midst for all of the people in the lake.

The all-including one caught up a man and gave White Corn Mother to him. This man he made the Town Chief, chief of the summer people. Then he caught up a second man and gave Ice Mother to him; he was made chief of the winter people.

In this manner the two-division system of a pueblo was established. The chief of the summer people is in charge of the summer months, and the chief of the winter people is in charge of the winter months. At the end of the respective seasons, the two chiefs transfer their authority. Seasonal transfers are a time of ceremonial observations.

Two little boys were created in Sand Lake, to be the little war gods, guardians of the people. They were supposed to think first like a man, then like a woman. They were sent up from the lake to report on what they saw. The people were getting ready what they would need to live in the world above.

When the boys returned they said, "Yes, we went up but we did not see any hills."

They were sent forth again, the younger ahead of the elder; then the elder ahead of the younger. They were told to shoot their arrows. The first arrow did not return, so that direction became north. More arrows were shot and, not returning, the directions were established and a color for each was named: north/blue, west/yellow, south/red, east/white, the zenith (up above)/speckled, and the nadir (down below)/black. Under water the Indians had no directions.

Pueblo prayer stick
After M. Stevenson, 1904

A sun symbol and two singers
behind an altar; lightning and rainbow design

Top, after J. W. Fewkes, 1919, pl. 87; bottom, after a painting, "Formation
of the Dance," by the late Abel Sanchez, Tewa Indian of San Ildefonso

"Now," the two little boys were told, "you have
to think like a woman. You have to put up the big
hills to the north." So they took a little adobe mud
and they threw it to the north.

Then they were told, "When we work, the sky
will get dark, there will be white clouds like a flower,
there will be a rainbow and lightning and the sound
of rain falling, and fog."

Tewa Buffalo Woman dancer

From an Indian painting in the Museum of New Mexico, Santa Fe

Tewa Buffalo Man Dancer

From a painting by an Indian artist in the Museum of New Mexico, Santa Fe

## The Journey

When the Tewa emerged from Sand Lake, at first they could not walk. When they began walking, some got headache and some got stomachache. They thought maybe the mothers they were carrying, the Ice Mother and the White Corn Mother, were not good mothers. A hunt chief opened their stomachs and found pointed things and stones there. He took out these bad things and put in good things such as turquoise and pink quartz.

They moved on, but they still had headache and stomachache. They still needed something. Then they knew they needed doctors. Four doctors were made. These were members of curing societies; they gave the people medicine.

They came to a big river. There Magpie was found. He put his long tail across the river and the guards passed over. The Old Ones, the summer and winter chiefs, came onto the other side. Then Magpie's tail turned over in the middle of the river and the people fell down into the water, where they were changed into fish. Thereafter the Tewa ate no fish.

But some were left on one side of the river, some on the other side. They called back and forth and threw stones and sticks at one another. Those that stayed on the one side were called Navajo, Apache, Ute, Kiowa, and Comanche Indians -- those who spoke other languages. To them the chiefs said, "You can build houses of deer and buffalo hide. When you have babies you will have deer meat to eat." Those on the other side stayed and built houses of adobe.

The chiefs walked on alone; they were very sorrowful. They said, "We need something," so they went back into Sand Lake. Then they brought some individuals called the Kóssa, who are members of a clown society. They made fun, and at last the people began to laugh and grow glad again.

*Kóssa*—Tewa priest-clown

From an Indian painting in the Museum of New Mexico, Santa Fe

Tewa Deer dancer

After a painting made by Encarnacion Peña, a Tewa Indian of San Ildefonso, when he was a young boy

# LEARNING FROM UNTOLD RECORDS

## Mud Heads and Fish Men

Since some of the Pueblo peoples of today are descended from the Old Ones, it is not surprising to find that hints of ancient myths and happenings exist. Not only do the Tewa have legends concerning people who fell into a stream and were turned into fish, but similar tales are found among other Pueblo Indians, such as the Zuñi. Also, petroglyphs on rock surfaces, and designs painted on walls of ceremonial chambers (kivas) show fish-men depictions. These are known to be centuries old.

A Mimbres bowl from southwestern New Mexico, dating to the 11th to 13th century, is decorated with two fishermen with lines entering the throat of a huge mythical fish. This being is clearly a human, bedecked with a fish mask and characteristic body features which cover all but an arm, leg, and foot.

At the ruin site of Kuaua, on the bank of the Rio Grande north of Albu-querque, New Mexico (Coronado State Monument), in a kiva dating in the 1400s, are painted murals. These display knobbed personages comparable to the Mud Heads of Zuñi and other pueblos. One, a dual being, especially displays fish-like features. And there also are fish-men personages, two, each a human whose head is engulfed by the major portion of a large fish body. The fact that they were painted horizontally, as fish would be swimming, adds to their fish-like character.

A Zuñi informant identified one of these personages as the Elder son of the Sun, and the other as the Younger son of Sun. The latter, as shown in the illustration here, is accompanied by hand symbols of the Twin War Gods, further indicating the duality so prominent among the Pueblos.

These instances give proof that myths extend far into the Indian past, and they demonstrate a wide spread of common concepts.

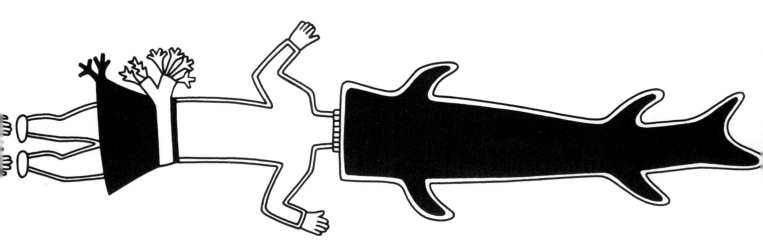

### A Kuana Fish-man
After B.P.Dutton 1963 : 180-81

Mimbres Fish-man pottery design (dating between A.D. 1050-1200)

From a pottery bowl in the University of Colorado Museum, Boulder

One of the Zuñi Mud Heads, known as the Wearer of the Eyelets of Invisibility, is knobbed like a warty, club-shaped squash. He never disappears, even when he thinks he does by hiding his head. He also has horns like a catfish.

Other Indian dancers, representing spirit beings, look even more like fish than the Mud Heads.

A Zuñi Mud Head, or *Kóyemshi*
After an Indian painting in the Museum of New Mexico, Santa Fe

A Kuana mural figure similar to a Zuñi Mud Head
After B.P.Dutton 1963: 180-181

The ceramic artists also devised intricate geometric designs for their vessels, especially on the smoothed interiors of bowls. Although these may not differ much, pueblo to pueblo, the Mimbres people used them and those with life form decoration primarily for a special purpose. When the Mimbres (who derive from a Mogollon culture base) buried their dead they "killed" the vessels so that the spirit of them and other valued possessions used in life could accompany the deceased to the under world, as typified by Wénima. Thus, most of the Mimbres decorated pottery recovered is found to have a small hole knocked through the vessel wall. Arrows are found broken, and other things shattered. From such burial habits, belief in afterlife is revealed. This proves that the Indians were religious people.

Importance of birds, animals—real and mythical—and numerous creatures is portrayed by a wide range of these in painted designs.

A Mimbres pottery design

After J.W. Fewkes, 1923: 46, Fig. 133

A dragon fly and a happy dancer, from Mimbres bowls
Left, after J. W. Fewkes, 1923; right, after O. T. Snodgrass, 1975.

## Rites and Practices Revealed

The representational paintings on pottery vessels offer opportunities for relating them to practices followed by Pueblo Indians of modern times. For instance, during the life of an Indian each one is given several names, certain of them being kept secret. The design of a Mimbres bowl shown here depicts two adults, one presumably a woman with a baby lying by her side and the other with ceremonial items and symbols indicating the enactment of naming rites for the baby.

From a Mimbres bowl
After O.T. Snodgrass, 1975 : 9 fig. 6

# BIBLIOGRAPHY

Bunzel, Ruth L. "Zuñi Kátcinas: an analytical study." *Bureau of American Ethnology Annual Report*, 47th Annual Report (1932):843-903.

Curtis, Edward S. *The North American Indian*, vol. I. 1907. 144 p., index, illus.

Curtis, Natalie. *The Indians' Book.* 1907. Reprint. New York: Dover Publications, 1968.

Cushing, Frank Hamilton. *Zuñi Breadstuff.* Reprint. New York: Museum of the American Indian, 1974.

Di Peso, Charles C. "The Upper Pima of San Cayetano del Tumacacori." *The Amerind Foundation*, Inc., No. 7.

Dutton, Bertha Pauline. *Sun Father's way; the Kiva murals of Kuaua; a Pueblo ruin, Coronado State Monument, New Mexico.* Albuquerque: University of New Mexico Press, 1963.

Fewkes, J. Walter. "Hopi Kátcinas, drawn by native artists." *Bureau of American Ethnology Annual Report*, 21st Annual Report (1903).

Fewkes, J. Walter. "Designs on prehistoric Hopi pottery." *Bureau of American Ethnology Annual Report*, 33rd Annual Report (1919):207-284.

Fewkes, J. Walter. "Designs on prehistoric pottery from the Mimbres Valley, New Mexico." *Smithsonian Miscellaneous Collections*, 74 (1923).

Haury, Emil W. *The Hohokam: Desert Farmers and Craftsmen.* Tucson: University of Arizona Press, 1976.

Lloyd, J. William. *Aw-aw-tam Indian Nights.* Westfield, New Jersey: The Lloyd Group, 1911.

Mangelsdorf, Paul C., MacNeish, Richard S., and Galinat, Walton C. "Prehistoric Wild and Cultivated Maize." *The Prehistory of the Tehuacan Valley*, Vol. I.:178-200. Austin: University of Texas Press, 1967.

Mindeleff, Victor. "A Study of Pueblo Architecture: Tusayan and Cibola." *Bureau of American Ethnology Annual Report*, Eighth Annual Report (1891):13-228.

Nequatewa, Edmund, "How the Hopi respect the game animals." *Hopi Customs, Folklore and Ceremonies*, Reprint Series No. 4: 32-33. Flagstaff: Museum of Northern Arizona, 1954.

Ogburn, Charlton, Jr. "The First Discovery of America." *Horizon* XLL, No. 1 (1970): 92-99.

Parsons, Elsie Clews. *The Pueblo of Jemez.* Andover, Massachusetts: Phillips Andover Academy, 1925.

Parsons, Elsie Clews. "Tewa Tales." *Memoir, American Folklore Society* Vol. 19 (1926).

Reichard, Gladys A. *Navajo Medicine Man.* New York: J.J. Augustin Publisher, 1939.

Robinson, A.E. (Bert). *The Basket Weavers of Arizona.* Albuquerque: University of New Mexico Press, 1954.

Russell, Frank. "The Pima Indians." *Bureau of American Ethnology Annual Report*, 26th Annual Report (1908).

Snodgrass, O.T. *Realistic Art and Times of the Mimbres Indians.* El Paso, Texas: Snodgrass, 1975.

Stephen, Alexander M. *Hopi Journal*, ed. E.C. Parsons. New York: Columbia University Contributions to Anthropology, Vol. 23, 1936.

Stevenson, Matilda Coxe. "The Zuñi Indians." *Bureau of American Ethnology Annual Report*, 23rd Annual Report (1904).

Underhill, Ruth Murray. *Singing for Power.* Berkeley: University of California Press, 1938.

Underhill, Ruth M. *The Papago Indians of Arizona and their Relatives the Pima.* Washington, D.C.: U.S. Office of Indian Affairs, Education Division, Sherman Pamphlets No. 3, 1940.

White, Leslie A. "The Acoma Indians." *Bureau of American Ethnology Annual Report*, 47th Annual Report (1929-30):17-192.